THE PEOPLE
VS
JAMAAL RUSS

2

DRUG RELATED

Table of Contents

Always See the Situation Clearly
Know What You Want
Expanding Possibilities
Evaluating and Deciding
Action

ALWAYS SEE THE SITUATION CLEARLY

It was the year everybody was talking about, Y2K, the year two thousand, the year the world was gonna blow-up. Jamaal was sixteen and introduced to the world of drugs. By the age of seventeen, Jamaal started to travel with his drug business to gain more capital at a faster rate and earn more money for a lesser quantity of product.

"Yo, Derek, ain't we catching the eight-thirty Shortline bus?"

Derek replied in a playful but funny voice. "And you know this man," "you know we can't miss that one." "Thousand-dollar Thursday tonight and then checks come out too." Jamaal and his friend Derek were preparing to go upstate Binghamton to sell crack cocaine. Thursday night in Binghamton was a great night for any dealer, even if you never sold drugs before.

Jamaal hated the idea of selling drugs only because there was a penalty behind it. Besides, the deeper you engage, the more severe the punishment could be. But knowing the hardship Jamaal's mother faced daily to support the immediate family, Jamaal felt he had no choice but to get it out the mud and try his best to lessen the buried life had installed on his moms.

"Yeah, boy, it's on and poppin'." We made it. "Thousand-dollar Thursday on pause for anybody that's on the block tonight." "Stop fronting, Derek, now you know Mack and her crew are gonna be on the block." "You love that girl, boy". "You know you're gonna let her run to every car that pulls up." Jamaal and Derek express their feelings and excitement on catching the eight-thirty bus to Binghamton. Before the bus pulled out, two white male Port Authority officers got onto the same Shortline bus headed to Binghamton that Jamaal and Derek was on.

Jamaal and Derek immediately made eye contact with each other. Derek immediately began to panic. Jamaal then asked Derek, "Yo, ya stuff put up?"

Derek responded, "Yeah."

The officers began to make an announcement as soon as they stepped foot on the bus, explaining why they were there. One of the officers then began to shout, "Everyone take your photo IDs out while my partner and I conduct an ID check. This process should not take long as long as we have everyone's undivided attention."

"Man, I have a misdemeanor warrant in Binghamton," Derek began to tell Jamaal.

Jamaal then replied, "Be easy, you good. We in NYC right now, if the warrant does pop up, they won't arrest you because Binghamton won't come down to pick you up." Jamaal was a little swift with the law so he would always keep calm by knowing the procedures.

While Jamaal and Derek sat patiently as the officers did their jobs, the officers started to come closer to the row where Jamaal and Derek were seated. Derek started to get even more nervous and suddenly stood up and began to make an attempt to get to the restroom. "Yo, what you doing? You can't wait? You can't hold it?" Jamaal asked.

Derek replied, "Hold what? I'm outta here".

The officers yelled in high-pitched voices while walking quickly towards Derek and Jamaal. While passing other passengers, they said, "Sit down, sit down now." Derek heard the voices and began to move at a faster speed towards the back of the bus, headed to the restroom. Upon

Derek making his getaway, the officers began to chase after him. Jamaal remained seated, watching as Derek tripped over another passenger's foot while running towards the back of the bus in that narrow aisle, just before where the restroom was located.

One of the officers jumped on top of Derek and immediately began to wrestle him, gaining a tight choke hold as if looking to make Derek tap out. Derek began to shout, "I can't breathe, I can't breathe!" while the other officer was placing handcuffs on him. When the officers picked Derek up from the middle of the aisle of the bus, one of the officers observed a ball wrapped in clear Reynolds plastic wrap drop from Derek's pants leg. The officer then screams in his high-pitched voice, "Hold him, hold him, I recovered something."

While the officers called backup they instructed everyone to stay in their seats. Upon the arrival of more officers, the two original officers then escorted Derek off the bus while the remaining officers continued the ID check. Derek's charge was originally obstruction of justice for interrupting the officers ID check, and resisting arrest for running and wrestling on the floor. But things changed once the officers noticed the drugs roll down Derek's pants leg; Derek was now in for a ride.

Jamaal felt irate and everything just seemed suspicious; he wanted to get off the bus at the next rest stop and take a cab back to Brooklyn, but he realized he didn't have enough money. Jamaal continued on with the four-hour bus trip to Binghamton with nothing to have faith in but God (Good Orderly Direction) himself, who rested inside of him. Jamaal would usually listen to music, but this ride he just couldn't do it. All he did was watch the passengers watch him.

Finally, the bus came to a rest stop and everyone got off the bus for a twenty-minute recess. Some passengers went to grab a bite to eat, some just stood around the bus and stretched their legs, and some went to the smoking section for a cigarette break. But Jamaal needed to calm his nerves. He was more leery after Derek's arrest, So Jamaal went to a little hidden area not too far from the bus, just enough distance to see the passengers reloading. Jamaal retrieved a piece of a rolled up blunt from his socks and lit it up while an unknown individual snapped photos of Jamaal from a distance.

KNOW WHAT YOU WANT

After a full week in Binghamton, Jamaal still hadn't met his quota. With so much to do back home in Brooklyn the upcoming week, Jamaal began to grow frustrated. For once he felt pressured, with having to attend the drug treatment program mandated by his parole officer and making his friend Derek's court appearance, not to mention Jamaal had to see his parole officer by the end of the week as well.

Jamaal decided to run specials for the local crackheads in the area. Jamaal cut his prices lower than every dealer that was hustling in the area. "Yo, Sparkles," Jamaal yelled out to one of the local junkies that ran all the dealers lots of money. "Look, I need you Sparkles."

"This better be good, boy. Whatcha got for me, baby?" Sparkles said to Jamaal.

"Sixty-forty. Every hundo you bring me you keep forty". Sparkles' eyes became real big and she began to thank Jamaal, telling him how grateful she was for such a deal. Jamaal then told Sparkles, "Look, I'm out here all night all morning, if you don't see me walking the block, I'll be at Deb's crib on James Street. Come there and I'll come out, blow the horn if you not walking cause you know how Deb be on acting."

Sparkles agreed with a cheesy grin on her face. Sparkles began to strut down the street, preying on her next victim so she could enjoy the sweet deal Jamaal had set in place for her. "Yooooo, Deb!" Jamaal called out to Deb from her back window. "Yo, Deb!" Jamaal still got no answer. Before

Jamaal could walk off, Deb moved the curtains slightly to see who was calling her. She recognized the voice but couldn't match the face.

Deb knew it was a dealer, which meant money most of the time, if not all the time. The dealers would come to Deb's house to bag up their product, bang a female, or simply just sit there while Deb ran her tricks all night just to buy crack. "Boy, what you want, I'm busy." "I got a dick in my face" "you got something", I'm gonna need a fifty when I'm done. "Is that a trick question, Deb?" asked Jamaal. "Yeah, I got something". I was going to chill for a minute, I'm gonna give you something extra. "Okay you can go in the back in the second room and don't let that scary ass white boy see you either." If you fuck up my money you're gonna pay me for that too".

When Deb's customers come through, most tricks are afraid of purchasing drugs or hanging with a prostitute, sometimes both when coming to the urban areas. They will automatically believe they were being set up to be robbed. Once the trick saw any suspicious movements that weren't part of the original plan when they first made contact with the prostitutes, plans usually failed; Deb didn't want that to happen so she warned Jamaal if it did he would have to pay that tab also. Jamaal sat in the back room counting his money and the remaining product he had left on his person. Still under pressure and on a time frame.

It had been a full hour with no signs of Sparkles, so Jamaal decided to take a walk to the store to see if Sparkles was anywhere in sight. "Yo, Deb, lock the door. I'll be back." Jamaal shouted out to Deb because he knew nobody was there but him and Deb; Deb was in her room alone and hitting her crack pipe. "Okay, I heard you, baby, be safe out there." Deb replied.

As Jamaal approached the store, there were a few other dealers that were loyal to the block just hanging out, gathered around and kicking the breeze. Jamaal knew each and every one of them. The boys were from Queens, NY. The boys and Jamaal had a good report with each other. It was a New York City bond called the BQE, referring to the Brooklyn Queens express train line back home in New York City. The BQE would run between Brooklyn and Queens back and forth daily. So, there was much respect for each other, no bad vibes, just a little friendly competition when it came to hustling on the block. "Yooooo, what's good boys? I see y'all out here getting fat while I starve," Jamaal jokingly played with the crowd of boys as he approached and recited a line from the movie *Kings Of New York*.

One of the boys replied, "Man you outta sight but not outta mind, we heard about that fire you got, the junkies keep looking specifically for you." As soon as he said that, Sparkles pulled up to the store in the passenger side of a white car with a white man driving. The car pulled into the parking lot and proceeded to a gas pump. Sparkles got out and began to head towards the crowd of dealers gathered by the store.

"Jay, I just came from Deb's looking for you. I got a hundred."

One of the dealers replied, "See? They are looking for you, champ."

We've been out here all day and they are screaming ya name. Jamaal remembered that Sparkles pulled into the store's parking lot with a white man in his car. Jamaal didn't want to serve Sparkles with any hand-to-hand interactions, so Jamaal told Sparkles he was going in the store and would be right back out. Jamaal went into the potato chip aisle and on the second shelf between the first two bags of Lay's chips he placed one hundred dollars' worth of his product.

Jamaal then walked to the counter with a bag of Lay's chips, paid for them and walked out the store. Jamaal walked back over to the crowd of dealers where Sparkles was standing and he told Sparkles to drop the one hundred dollar bill on the ground and to go in the store to the potato chip aisle, and on the second shelf between the first two bags of Lay's chips it's all there. Jamaal picked up the bill and continued to mingle with the other dealers while Sparkles went to retrieve the product she had just purchased from Jamaal.

"Thank you, baby." Sparkles said to Jamaal while exiting the store and walking towards the gas pump where the white man she pulled up with was parked.

One of the guys from Queens had pulled Jamaal to the side and had asked Jamaal if he could buy some of the product Jamaal was selling. Jamaal was thinking about it; he knew that move could get him back to Brooklyn sooner, but it would shorten his pockets. Jamaal had no plans of selling any weight to any one this trip; he promised himself he would stick to breaking down his product to maximize his profit.

Before Jamaal could answer "no" to the guys question, the store was rushed by The City of Binghamton police department, demanding all the individuals standing there put their hands up and didn't move. One of the officers began to give orders to the individuals. "Everyone stand side-by-side, this won't take long. We received a call about people hanging out in front of this storefront selling drugs, so we're gonna frisk search everyone and as long as you're clean, you're free to go."

Nobody ever just kept drugs in their plain old pocket while standing on the block. So, when the officer said frisk search and not cavity search everyone felt relieved. A cavity search would have consisted of everybody going to the precincts and being stripped searched. All the boys were dirty, including Jamaal. But Jamaal had a way around that too if things had led up to that point and gotten out of hand.

After Jamaal and the boys were searched, they were told to get off the store's property. Jamaal was deep in thought about this trip and felt enough was enough and to take the guy up on his offer and sell him the remaining product he had left so he could catch the next bus back to New York City, even though he wouldn't meet his quota.

EXPANDING POSSIBILITIES

"Docket number 2007bk1693 defendant is incarcerated with a hold," said the court officer. Jamaal was en route to his friend Derek's court matter held in lower Manhattan at 111 Centre Street. Jamaal had just made it into the court building out of breath as if he was running for his life as the court officer called Derek's docket number.

Jamaal waited for the elevator in the courthouse lobby to head to the courtroom where Derek's case was being heard. Derek's attorney had gotten a text message and after reading the text message, Mr. Railroad asked the judge if he could approach the bench. The judge agreed and Mr. Railroad and the district attorney began to walk towards the judge's bench.

The judge then shouted out to the courts officers who were escorting Derek out of the hold pen in the back. "Hold the next case. Leave Mr. Star in the holding cell for a fifteen-minute recess." As soon as the judge uttered them words, Jamaal came storming into a half empty courtroom still a little out of breath. Jamaal went straight to the guardrail where the clerk was sitting and signaled to the court clerk.

"Excuse me, miss, excuse me. Did they call Derek Star's case?"

"No, sir, you can have a seat. That case is the next one on our docket. In fact, there are the attorneys for that matter standing at the bench. Mr. Derek Star's attorney is the one with the navy blue suit. The other gentleman is the lead district attorney for the matter."

Jamaal went to speak to Derek's attorney. "Hello, sir, my name is Jamaal Russ and I'm here on behalf of Derek Star."

"Well, hello, Mr. Russ. My name is Mr. Railroad, and, as you already know, I represent Derek in this matter. Today is Derek's one eighty day. This is the day–" But before Derek's attorney could finish his sentence, Jamaal cut him off and finished it for him. "Sir, there must be a preliminary hearing or grand jury action taken by the DA in your case within 120 hours of your arrest, or within 5 days or 144 hours if there is a weekend or holiday occurring during confinement."

Mr. Railroad looked amazed after Jamaal said those words to him so swiftly. Mr. Railroad went on to say, "Well, unfortunately, Mr. Russ, Derek waived his rights at the arraignment hearing when he was initially booked on these charges and was just here today to set a date for his supreme court hearing, which should be two months from today."

Jamaal went on to say, "Yeah, I understand, sir. With your help, I'm pretty sure Derek would do something like that." The attorney made a strange face and immediately moved to end the conversation. "Mr. Russ, we have to get back inside so the case can be called."

"Docket number 2000bk3017 defendant is incarcerated and produced before this court with a hold," said the court officer. It was a normal procedure for the court officers of any court to read off the defendant statues on record to the court. In Derek's matter, he had a hold; a hold was when there is another jurisdiction that Derek had to answer to before thinking about ever being released on any type of conditions in the court he was currently facing. Until Derek answered to whatever it was that the jurisdiction set a warrant out for Derek's arrest for, he couldn't be released.

Jamaal sat directly in front on the first bench to be sure to see Derek when he came out to stand in front of the judge.

As soon as Derek walked out, Jamaal signaled to Derek and said in a whisper, "Yo, tell the judge you wanna go to the grand jury." Jamaal repeated it again as Derek walked out with a grin from ear to ear, happy and shocked to see Jamaal in court for him, nobody but Jamaal.

Jamaal wasn't sure if Derek heard him or not, but Derek was now in front of the judge and Mr. Railroad was speaking. "Your Honor, this matter is scheduled for grand jury proceedings today and my client–"

Before Mr. Railroad could finish his opening statement, Derek said in a loud voice, "I wanna grand jury."

The judge lifted his head up from writing and asked, "Council, did your client say something?" Mr. Railroad started to stutter.

"Excuse me, Your Honor, I'm not sure what my client's remark was. May we have a minute?"

Derek then said it again, not knowing what it meant but just repeating the words Jamaal muttered to him. "I wanna grand jury."

The judge then asked Derek, "You mean you want to go to the grand jury?" Derek replied yes. Derek looked behind him and caught eyes with Jamaal.

Jamaal whispered to Derek, "You good, I'm gonna holla at you." Jamaal got up to exit the courtroom. The judge then hit his gavel and stated to the courts.

"The defendant is remanded for two o'clock grand jury action at the supreme court building. Bail conditions remain fifty thousand no bond. Defendant has a warrant in another jurisdiction."

Mr. Railroad was now angry because he knew he was in for a longer evening and it was Friday. Derek didn't know what just happened, all he knew was that he did what Jamaal told him to do. While Derek was being escorted back to the holding pen, he asked the court officer a series of questions about his case. "When do I come back to court? Is my bail the same? What about my warrant?" The court officer, a young black male freshly out of the academy and full of care and concern, replied to Derek's series of questions.

"You don't have a court date, as of now your case is going in front of the grand jury today. You have the option to testify on your behalf if you choose to. As for your bail conditions, yes it's the same, fifty thousand. You also have a warrant in another jurisdiction you have to answer to." With Derek still a little confused, he was placed in the cell to await transportation to the supreme court building for his grand jury proceedings.

Jamaal was already in lower Manhattan and just a few stops away on the number three train from Jay Street Borough Hall where he had to attend his drug treatment program. Jamaal was eager to hurry up and finish with the program so he could go to his mom's apartment, which was located in the Brownsville section of Brooklyn. There, Jamaal would kick it with his siblings, if they were home at the time, while he waited on however long it may take to get his hands on the new product to go back out of town with.

"Yooooooo, Brody, I'm in town at my mom's crib. I need that same smack or something better, kid." Jamaal was talking on his mom's house phone to an old classmate named Pedro he would get his product from. "Where you at? How long's it gonna take to get to me?"

"Man, to be honest, I won't be back until tomorrow. I'm up in Buffalo." Pedro replied.

Jamaal answered, "Okay, cool, no sweat. Just call this number here when you come back. I'll be here."

It was just a little past five thirty and Jamaal was fast asleep on his mom's sofa in the living room. *Knock knock knock.* The loud noise awoke Jamaal and he jumped up as if he was having a bad dream. "Somebody get the door!" Came a loud roar from the back of the apartment. It was Jamaal's sister, who rarely came out of her room.. As Jamaal's little brother was opening the door, Jamaal looked at the clock on the wall only to realize it was after five o'clock and he didn't make it to see his parole officer.

"Fuck! Damn, I knew I shouldn't've went to sleep." Jamaal's older brother walked in the house.

"What you screaming for? Relax, can't be that bad." Jamaal looked at his older brother with a disgusting look on his face.

"Boy, I missed parole today, I overslept."

"Oh yeah, that's something to scream about." While Jamaal's older brother walked towards the back of the house, he asked, "So, what you gonna do?"

Jamaal replied, "I don't know yet, but I'll figure something out."

Jamaal had a few options, not many, but at least two. Jamaal could report on Monday morning and explain to his parole officer what had happened and prepare himself for a urine sample at his parole officer's request. Plus sign a document stating that his parole officer warned him about when he failed to report. Jamaal's other option was to just not report anymore.

Jamaal sat on his mom's sofa weighing the two options. He knew his urine was dirty and signing the document for the failure to report would be the second document he signed within ninety days due to the curfew violation he had received a month back. Jamaal wasn't too worried about the dirty urine for the weed cause he was in a drug treatment program. The drug program protected Jamaal from a violation for weed as long as Jamaal attended the program and showed progress, which Jamaal made it his business to do.

Jamaal really wasn't trying to gamble with his life, but he was looking at an easy one year in state prison for a parole violation. One of Jamaal's biggest fears was to go back to prison with nothing established to come back home to, so Jamaal wasn't taking no chances with the parole system and how they operated. Jamaal decided to not report back to parole. He was gonna wait on that phone call tomorrow from Pedro and immediately head back to Binghamton to sell crack cocaine.

EVALUATING AND DECIDING

At the last count at eleven o'clock p.m., which was a standard procedure that the jail would perform every night, the correction officer told Derek that once the count cleared, to pack up his belongings and that he was being bailed out. Derek was totally confused; he had only come from court around eight o'clock that night after sitting in the ball pens all day, tired and hungry. Derek refused to close his eyes around a bunch of other inmates, or eat any of those cheese sandwiches beginning served with a small carton of milk that was usually served in a school setting. Things didn't get any better after not seeing anyone after his first initial appearance in front of the judge early that day, when he saw Jamaal. Derek began to question the correction officer, as if the officer had made a mistake, he thought the officer had the wrong inmate.

"I know how to do my job. Your name is Derek Star, correct? Your booking case number is 141-678-1693, correct'? Pack up unless you wanna stay here. The count shouldn't take no more than an hour. Another officer is coming to get you to escort you to intake to process your release." The officer said.

Derek replied "Okay," and began to walk to his cell in disbelief. Lots of things were going through Derek's head at that very moment. Derek had seen plenty of jail movies where an inmate escaped or was released by accident. But never did he expect to believe that may be his situation one day. Derek sat on the metal rail bed in his cell and started to think that maybe they were making a mistake with his case.

Derek knew there wasn't anybody in their right mind that would pay a fifty grand bail to get him out.

Back at his mom house, Jamaal laid on the sofa deep in thought; it was two o'clock in the morning and for some reason, Jamaal just couldn't close his eyes to fall asleep. So, he decided to walk to the neighborhood's corner bodega to see if any of the weed dealers were still out serving. Unfortunately, there was no one in sight at the bodega, so Jamaal started to walk towards the train station. The train station was a little further, and Jamaal was sure to get weed from the twenty-four-hour weed spot the Jamaicans had owned and operated for years on Linden Ave.

As the train pulled into the station at Sutter Ave in the Brownsville section of Brooklyn, Derek was so eager and desperate to get off the train. He had to pee so badly, he started to pull his penis out in the train car while the train was in motion, but there were too many passengers. The train doors opened, and Derek immediately hurled himself to a corner on the platform of the train's station and urinated with much relief.

Jamaal just had purchased a ten-dollar sack of weed and was eager to get back to his mom's house to sit on the sofa and get wasted and wait on the call from Pedro. As Jamaal approached the first bodega he realized he didn't have any blunt to roll the weed in. Just before entering the bodega, Jamaal heard his name in a loud shout and immediately recognized the voice. Derek was walking from the train station and spotted Jamaal walking out of the weed spot. Derek was unsure it was Jamaal at first due to the dimness of lights in that particular area, so he picked up his walking speed. Then, he began to jog until he reached the block where the bodega was located, which had more lights; when he could finally see clearly that it was Jamaal, he called out to him.

"Yoooooooo, Jay! Yooooo, Jay!" Jamaal turned around before entering the bodega with a grin on his face. When Derek reached Jamaal, they greeted each other with a hand gesture and a hug and Jamaal replied, "Yo wassup, Playa Boy. I see you took my word of advice this time around."

Derek had a grateful look on his face, Derek looked at Jamaal as if Jamaal was the one that just bailed him out of jail. "What do you mean?" Derek asked Jamaal as they both exited the bodega and began to walk back towards the apartment buildings where Jamaal's mom stayed.

Jamaal began to explain to Derek about the grand jury proceedings. "Remember what you said to the judge in court?"

Derek remembered immediately. "Yeah, some grand jury bullshit. What the fuck was that about?"

Jamaal replied, "Boy, that's the reason why you here talking to me now. You and I both know ain't nobody paying no 50k for ya ass." Jamaal started to laugh, and added, "unless you snitched on somebody."

Before Derek could say anything to explain to Jamaal what had happened, Jamaal interrupted him. "Man, I already know what happened, I probably can tell you better than you can remember. it's a system we in and just a process you just experienced."

Jamaal then went on and asked Derek, "did you testify in front of the grand jury? Or did you just sit in the holding pen, until the last Rikers Island bus back to the jail?"

Derek replied to Jamaal's questions with no hesitation. "Man, I sat in that cell all tired and hungry and I didn't see anybody."

"Yeah, that's a good thing. I was hoping you didn't because whatever you would have said would have stuck with you and been used at your trial, if you don't take a plea deal.

But when the district attorney is not ready to produce their witness the grand jury action is usually postponed and charged to the people, and in those cases they release the defendant on their 180.80 motion pending grand jury action." But Derek had lied to Jamaal. He had made a grand jury appearance and testified. In exchange for Derek's testimony, he was promised a release date from one of his arresting officers.

"Man, those people crazy. They forever tryna lynch a black man alive. But good looking, bro, I appreciated you looking out for me. But, yo, Jay, I need to get right now, this jail shit fucked me up this time around. Gonna need help to get back on my feet. when you are going back up top?" Derek asked.

"I'm waiting on something now, I should have it today." Jamaal answered.

Derek walked Jamaal to his mom's building and once they reached the building, Jamaal and Derek each made a hand gesture toward one another and began to part ways. "Yo, Derek, make sure when you get up you come straight to my mom's crib."

Derek agreed and replied back, "Yeah, I'm going to my baby mom's crib. You know ya boy ain't have no pussy in a week, I'm horny as a mother fucker." Derek and Jamaal both laughed at the comment Derek had just made as they walked separate ways from each other.

It was twelve o'clock noon on a nice sunny Saturday and Jamaal was still waiting for that phone call from Pedro. Jamaal didn't wanna leave his mom's apartment and miss the call, but he wanted to go outside and enjoy the weather. Suddenly, there was a knock at the door. As Jamaal started to walk towards the door to answer it, the phone rang at the same time. "Who is it?" Jamaal called, trying to figure out who was at the door while he was also running to answer the cordless house phone .

"It's me, bro, Derek." Came the reply.

"Okay, hold on, Dee." Jamaal replied.

As Jamaal skipped back over to the door and looked through the peep hole to confirm it was Derek, he answered the ringing phone at the same time. "Hello, who this?" On the other end of the phone was Jamaal's guy, Pedro. The call Jamaal was waiting for.

As soon as Derek came into the apartment, he nodded at Jamaal's little brother who was playing a hand-held video game in the living room. Derek flopped onto the sofa as if he had had a long night while Jamaal finished up on the phone. "Okay, cool, five minutes I'll be downstairs."

Jamaal hung up the phone very excitedly; he reached over to Derek and they high-fived. "Yo, I be right back, 'bout to run downstairs and get that."

Derek asked Jamaal if he wanted him to come. But Jamaal knew Pedro didn't like two things: talking on a cellphone and meeting new faces. So, Jamaal told Derek he was good and it wouldn't take him long to return.

ACTION

Derek was ready to put his plan into action. Once Jamaal left his mom's apartment, Derek asked Jamaal's little brother if he could use the bathroom. When Derek reached the bathroom, he pulled out a cell phone and began to dial numbers. Derek sat on the toilet as he talked to the person on the other end of the phone. "Yes, we on our way up there." "He's getting the work now." "Yes, sir, yes sir." "No, I don't know how much it is, sir." "Okay, I will. Goodbye, sir."

Jamaal came back into the apartment excited. Derek was sitting on the sofa in the same spot he was when Jamaal left to meet his connection downstairs. Jamaal skipped straight to the back of the apartment to prepare for the trip. While hurtling to the back, he yelled out to Derek on the sofa. "Yo, Dee, I'm getting ready to see what the bus schedule looks like."

Derek shouted out, "Okay," while Jamaal went into a back room with the cordless phone and closed the door.

"Hello, what's the next bus to Binghamton?" While Jamaal was on the phone, he was also separating his crack and placing it into a balloon. This time, Jamaal planned to hold all the work until they reached Binghamton before he would give Derek the portion he had promised him. Jamaal also planned to booth the produce this time, just in case. So Jamaal greased his ass crack and pushed the balloon up his rectum until it disappeared. Jamaal would have to sit on a toilet and move his bowels in order to retrieve his product.

When Jamaal came from the back of the apartment, Derek asked if everything was good.

Jamaal replied, "You already know I have your portion for you also," Before Jamaal could tell Derek that he would give him his portion once they had reached Binghamton, Derek told Jamaal he didn't need the handout anymore. Derek pulled out a wad of hundreds and said his baby mom robbed some trick the other day and she looked out for him; once they reached Binghamton, he could in fact purchase some of the product Jamaal just purchased for himself.

After Derek turning down Jamaal's offer, Jamaal called a cab on his mom's cordless house phone to take him and Derek to the Port Authority bus station on 42nd Street in Manhattan. While Jamaal and Derek were in the cab, Derek kept complaining about how bad he had to urinate. Jamaal told Derek that once they got to the station, he'd get the tickets and Derek could go to the restroom. After, they would link back up in the line to board the bus.

Once the cab pulled in front of the Port Authority, Jamaal and Derek got out of the cab and began their mission. Jamaal headed towards the ticket booth and Derek went to the restroom in a hurry. When he got away from Jamaal, he quickly made a phone call. "Sir, we are here, we are at the Port Authority." "At the ticket booth." The person on the other end of the phone had asked Derek where Jamaal was located. After Derek muttered the words, he immediately hung up the cell phone.

After purchasing the tickets, Jamaal turned around to make his way towards the bus. Jamaal then noticed the individual who was mysteriously looking at him the day Derek was arrested, when Jamaal had gotten off the bus and ducked off to the side for a smoke break when he became nervous. This time, the individual was with two other white men.

"Jamaal Russ, freeze right there, we have a warrant to search you and your belongings." Jamaal dropped the knapsack on the marble floor as he complied with the Port Authority officers while they conducted their search of him and his belongings. The officers escorted Jamaal to a search room located on the lower level. While Jamaal was being escorted, he swiveled his head to see if Derek was in sight, but to no avail. Jamaal made it all the way to the search room with no signs of Derek.

Derek was at his baby mom's apartment awaiting for the arrival of the mysterious individual, the officer who had been watching Jamaal on his smoke break the day of Derek's arrest. Derek had to return the cell phone and be updated on safety measures after just snitching on Jamaal, with no arrest being made. The officer was present at the Port Authority and was a part of the search conducted on Jamaal a few days ago.

It's been a full day and Jamaal still hadn't moved his bowels. Jamaal was at Deb's house trying to retrieve his product that was clogged in his system. He was exhausted; he was finally back in Binghamton after nearly escaping a one-way ticket to jail. "Yo, mama Deb, do you have some laxative? You know, the stuff to clean your system out and make you shit." Jamaal asked Deb.

"Nah, baby, but they carry it at the bodega up the block." Deb answered.

"Okay, Deb, thanks. You want me to get you something since I'm going?"

"Yeah, baby, bring be a beer."

Jamaal headed out to the bodega to get some laxative and a beer for Deb. Before Jamaal could reach the bodega, a detective car pulled up next to him as he was walking. Two officers in suits jumped out and told Jamaal to place his hands behind his back and that he was under arrest and had a sealed indictment issued by the city of Binghamton for criminal sale of a controlled substance in the third degree.

Jamaal knew something was different and it wouldn't just be a week in jail when he heard the officer say the words "sealed indictment". Jamaal had heard those words before and knew that the grand jury proceedings had taken place already, in secret, with him not having any knowledge of it. So, apparently, the city of Binghamton felt they had a solid case against Jamaal.

Ten months later, Jamaal was still being housed at the Binghamton county jail awaiting trial on a class B felony criminal sale of a controlled substance in the third degree. Jamaal was also serving a parole violation for a term of one year; his parole officer came to serve him his violation papers for failure to report just a week after Jamaal was arrested on his new charges.

Jamaal had a court date set soon at the county courthouse in Binghamton. The pre-trial hearings were set to start soon. Ms. Rosure, who represented Jamaal, was a short white lady with blonde hair who always seemed to have cold-like symptoms; she would sniffle a lot and play with her nose. Ms. Rosure would also flirt often with the district attorney who was handling Jamaal's case, Mr. Smith, during the court proceedings.

Ms. Rosure and Mr. Smith entered Judge Mathews' courtroom minutes before Jamaal's hearing was scheduled to start. Judge Mathews told both attorneys to approach his bench. Upon their approach, Judge Mathews began to speak.

"Now we all Know Mr. Russ's parole terms are coming to an end soon." I want this case prosecuted swiftly as possible. I don't want to allocate any of the county's funds on this matter when the state is gladly paying the county now to house this perp. Let's get this conviction so he can go back to the state where he belongs." All three parties agreed with devilish looks on their faces, As Mr. Smith and Ms. Rosure walked off to their opposite sides of the courtroom.

It was Jamaal's Wade hearing. The purpose of a Wade hearing is to determine whether the eyewitness's identification of the defendant as the perpetrator of the crime is correct. Jamaal was charged with selling a quantity of crack cocaine to an individual. Jamaal had knowledge of the situation but didn't remember how it actually played out at that moment.

"Your Honor, we the people would like to call Officer Frembrez to the stand." A white man with blue eyes and sandy blond hair, about six foot four, came walking out from the back. He had never seen him a day in his life; at least, that's what Jamaal thought.

"Mr. Frembrez, were you working in your official capacity as an undercover police officer at nine p.m. on Thursday, September 4th of this year?"

"Yes, Sir, Yes."

"And were you alone?"

"No, sir, I wasn't."

"Mr. Frembrez, do you recall driving into a parking lot of a bodega and parking at a gas pump?"

"Yes, Sir, I do."

Jamaal then realized what this was about. "Sparkles," Jamaal said to himself. Sparkles was with an undercover cop the night she purchased the one-hundred-dollars-worth of product from Jamaal. But Jamaal knew they didn't have much, because he didn't serve Sparkles hand-to-hand.

But, then again, Jamaal had to remember what battlefield he was on. It's not where you are from, it's where you are at that matters. Binghamton was dirty; their conviction rate was ninety-eight percent; most dealers, if not all, took a plea bargain during their first week incarcerated in Binghamton. All Mr. Smith needed from this hearing to get a trial date and possible conviction with an all-white jury was for Officer Frembrez to say that he observed Jamaal serve crack cocaine that night.

"Officer Frembrez, do you see the person you observed selling crack cocaine the night of September 4th?"

"Ummmm. They all look the same, I'm not sure if it's that one."

Jamaal immediately tapped Ms. Rosure, telling her to make an objection right now and move for a dismissal. Jamaal knew he had to get that on record just in case he had to fight this case on an appeal. Ms. Rosure started to stutter in a scary tone while muttering the words, "Objection, Your Honor".

Judge Mathews dropped his pen and replied in an annoyed tone of voice, "Objection sustained. Case adjourned, be back here in the same court four weeks from today." Mr. Smith was furious now that he had to work extra hard if he wanted to secure this victory. Mr. Smith would somehow need to get a hold of Sparkles and make her drop dime on Jamaal. Mr. Smith had no identification on the perpetrator and had four weeks before Judge Mathews had to dismiss the case by law.

One day before his new court date, Jamaal had been locked up for eleven months and hasn't spoken to anybody in his family. Jamaal was in the recreation room writing a letter to his moms, informing her that he was okay and that he was in jail for something and might be home soon.

"Jamaal Russ, counsel visit." The correction officer yelled out on the microphone. Jamaal was surprised to receive a counsel visit. This was something unheard of.

Ms. Rosure came to the jail to relay the message the district attorney Mr. Smith had for Jamaal, regarding a last-minute plea bargain agreement. Jamaal wasn't into taking any plea, not now nor ever did it cross his mind during the whole court proceedings.

"Mr. Russ, Mr. Smith is willing to reduce the charges to a class C felony. Not to mention he wants to offer you time served, which will run concurrent with your parole violation and you will go home on your expected date, which is in four weeks."

Jamaal replied in a soft, casual tone of voice, "Mr. Rosure, I kindly will refuse Mr. Smith's offer. After the way the hearing turned out, I'd rather take my chances picking a jury."

Ms. Rosure then went on to say, "Well, you know now that Mr. Smith is preparing to produce a confidential informant and that will really hurt our case."

"Okay, Ms. Rosure. It was a pleasure speaking with you, but I need to get back to writing my letter to my family." Jamaal then got up and walked towards the guard to escort him back to his housing unit.

Ms. Rosure left the jail and retrieved her property. She immediately pulled her cell phone from her purse and began to dial Mr. Smith's phone number. "He's not going for it." She told him.

"Fuck!" Mr. Smith shouted on the other end of the phone. Mr. Smith continued, "Mathews is gonna dismiss this case. I can't produce the informant and we didn't get a positive ID from the Wade hearing." The phone then went to a dial tone as Mr. Smith hung up on Ms. Rosure.

As soon as he made it to the housing unit, within the first few hours at the jail, Jamaal laid in his cell reminiscing about the time he ran into Sparkles. Sparkles was sentenced to five days in jail for getting caught trespassing and having a crack stem on her. Sparkles was housed in the female unit across from Jamaal and they were able to communicate with each other through their personal vents in their cells. Sparkles was thirsty to get high once Jamaal told Sparkles he hadn't shitted in two days and what he had in him. Sparkles was excited and immediately faked sick that evening just to go to the infirmary to get the laxative for Jamaal. Sparkles told Jamaal to keep a look out for the guy with the glasses from his unit that goes out to receive his medication from the infirmary every day. She said that the guy would have the laxative to give to Jamaal once he returns from the infirmary.

"Court walking out! Court walking out!" The correction officer shouted out to the inmates who had a court appearance schedule that morning. Once Jamaal's bus arrived at the courthouse, his case was the first case to be called.

"In the matter of The People Vs Jamaal Russ, I, Judge Mathews, here by dismiss all said charges against the defendant. The defendant remains in the care and custody of correction to finish out the remainder of his state parole terms. This county releases all jurisdiction on Mr. Russ as he awaits the state to return him to the state to finish his term." The Judge hit the gravel and said the case was dismissed. Jamaal was now officially on the countdown to becoming a free man again.

The time finally came for Jamaal's release. That morning, he woke up super early and was going from cell to cell, passing out belongings he would no longer need any more. Everyone was grateful to see Jamaal leaving. But, of course, there's always one bad apple out of the bunch. One of the inmates yelled out "HE'LL BE BACK." Jamaal heard the shout and didn't even turn around, he just kept walking and shaking his head.

Jamaal was set free.

"Some things never change" would be a perfect phrase to end this story on. Our protagonist is vindicated. The "evil" powers that be, if only for a moment, had met their comeuppance. The rebels had fought against the empire and won. But, like always, one solitary victory was not enough to change the torrential tides.

We live in a new era of greater understanding. Today can be a different kind of victory. If we have the fortitude and the faith to hold what we know to be true, we can accomplish anything. We are more connected, and more readily available to enact social change than ever before.

It was time for Jamaal to make right on his promises to influence others in a positive way. With his story, Jamaal would be the one to break barriers and be more than just a single statistic. He could dedicate his life to broadening society's expectations.

May we all have the energy within us to do the same.